THE KILLING OF OSAMA BIN LADEN:

How the Mission to Hunt Down a Terrorist Mastermind was Accomplished

MARK YOSHIMOTO NEMCOFF

ISBN: 1-934602-18-3
ISBN-13: 978-1-934602-18-8

Published by Glenneyre Press, LLC.
Los Angeles, CA
www.wordsushi.com

Third Edition

Cover design by: MYN

Praise for
THE KILLING OF OSAMA BIN LADEN

"I would bet there will be phones ringing at the Pentagon or inside the Beltway once word of this book gets out...if you are looking for a highly informative and thrilling rendition of how the man Hunt for Osama bin Laden unfolded, definitely look no further than this one."
- STEVE SAMBLIS - ICPlaces.com Book Reviews

TABLE OF CONTENTS:

MAY 1, 2011

I turned on the TV and saw him there, the boy in the tree. Outward he glanced, his face struck with a sense of jubilation and awe as he and a growing throng by the edge of the fence gazed toward the White House. Men, women and children had come to the home of the President of the United States to wave the flag, be together and feel good about being Americans at a time when it seemed a damn bit too long since there had been reason to celebrate anything.

They had emerged in droves from hotels and townhouses nearby. Several Georgetown students sprinted down Pennsylvania Avenue shouting, "U.S.A! U.S.A!" In a way, it seemed like Christmas Day and New Year's Eve all wrapped up into one.

Osama Bin Laden, the criminal mastermind behind the September 11, 2001 attacks that destroyed the World Trade Center and killed thousands of innocent civilians, the man who epitomized evil in this world, was dead.

There was no way to measure the surprise felt by America on the night of May 1, 2011 other than to look out into the streets and see those faces lit up with glee. I have no doubt the volume of beers being poured in bars and taverns across the country reached a peak not seen since the U.S. Olympic Hockey Team pulled off the Miracle on Ice back in Lake Placid some three decades earlier.

At front and center of the world's consciousness, for the moment at least, was the sense that we had finally put a big W in the win column for once. Our military expansion across the globe into regions most Americans had never heard of had caused one of the many rifts tearing this country apart. The financial cost of the War on Terror paled in comparison to the loss of all those young American lives— those bright futures that would never be realized because of a crusade to end the state of fear this country had been plunged into on that dark September morning back in 2001.

For a decade it all seemed for nothing. A waste beyond the imagination. A war for oil. An exercise in futility.

Color coded terror alerts became the norm. Travel became a ridiculous hassle. I can barely remember what it was like to wear shoes through the airport without having to take them off. Extensive pat downs akin to molestation and full body scanning made us feel more violated than safe.

The world had changed so much, so fast; none for the better. We had gone headlong into a downward spiral of Orwellian proportions. If the terrorist's aim was to disrupt our lives and resources by plunging our country into a state of perpetual fear then it seemed like the damned terrorists were winning.

However, all of that changed on May 1, 2011 in a little-known garrison town, deep behind the Pakistani borders, and in plain view of the whole world. The manhunt for the criminal who had stolen our safety away from us was now over, setting off the collective sigh heard 'round the world. We had put Osama Bin Laden on the night train to the big adios.

Navy SEALs got the murdering bastard, putting a hot round into his skull for good measure.

U.S. Intelligence sources sifted through nearly a decade's worth of raw data accumulated from the repeated questioning of detainees. Once and for all, they had been able to pinpoint where America's top enemy had been hiding. This ridiculous cat-and-mouse game was finally over. We were able to finally show that nobody takes our cheese and gets out of this place alive.

Really, it couldn't have happened to a nicer guy and Americans knew it. Outside the White House gates, a large group within the growing crowd burst into an impromptu version of "The Star Spangled Banner" as the rest of the world watched on TV and awaited news on how the most significant story of the Twenty-first century had come to be. In New York City, whose very history will forever be intertwined and tainted by the shadow of the most unspeakable monster in a generation, Times Square and the streets near Ground Zero erupted with the voices of people screaming "God Bless America" as tears welled up in their eyes.

The Internet was virtually choked with traffic. Twitter users and Facebook friends alerted the world to the news and basked in the comfort of community.

Those lost would never be forgotten. Somewhere, the heroes of 9/11 were smiling down upon us because, finally, we had gotten the pathetic fool who dared to try to break our indomitable spirit.

MANHUNT

Nearly a decade after the September 11, 2001 terrorist attacks made him the most wanted fugitive on the planet, we still hadn't apprehended Osama Bin Laden. A price had been put on his head and a blank check written by our government to fund his capture. The promise had been made to every citizen of the United States whose lives were forever changed by the deeds of a false prophet masquerading as the messenger of God's will.

We will get him...became our mantra. Deep in our hearts as Americans, we knew justice would be meted out for these heinous crimes. Sonofabitch was going to pay.

Then somehow, over time, though our national resolve had only slightly wavered, our hunger to bring the bad guy to justice had gone from full-blown fervor to a faded bumper sticker. His name had certainly not been forgotten, least of all by those who still remembered the sick feeling of watching the events of that dark September morning, but somehow the flame had burned dim. Our reason to continue sending troops to Muslim countries that certainly didn't appear to want us there seemed clouded at best.

We had lost sight of the target. Instead of the constant demonizing one particular Muslim, the absence of Bin Laden from the public eye began to birth a climate in parts of this country where it just seemed natural to demonize all Muslims.

Even those who were natural born, law-abiding American citizens.

The damage to the American psyche caused by the inability to locate Bin Laden was enormous. If the only people with the resources to do the job, couldn't, then who would protect us, the little people?

It wasn't for lack of desire on our government's part that Bin Laden had not been quickly apprehended, but more because Osama Bin Laden had again taken to the wind, a practice he had perfected while fighting the Soviets in the mountains of Afghanistan during the 1980s. One minute he was supposedly in this place or that place, and then the next moment he wasn't. Osama Bin Laden had become harder to find than Waldo in a candy cane factory.

Sporadic news updates over the last decade placed Bin Laden in the rugged terrain of the mountainous Tora Bora region along the Afghan/Pakistani border. A barely regulated, mostly autonomous zone of impossibly rocky hills and mountains, Tora Bora offered unspeakably bad weather and plenty of opportunities to use up precious resources and human lives searching through a nearly endless labyrinth of caverns. The caves had been utilized since ancestral times to help tribal warriors fight off foreign invaders, but by 2001 were electrified with hydro-electric power harnessed from running streams. For this, Bin Laden had the United States to thank. The entire multi-level cave complex had been fortified, in part, by the CIA to help the Mujahideen during the Soviet invasion of Afghanistan.

Back in mid-December 2001, when the wounds of 9/11 were still quite fresh, U.S. Army forces fighting in Tora Bora came within two thousand meters of Bin Laden, only to see him slip away into Pakistan. There he took an easterly route through snow-covered mountains to the area of Parachinar. Gary Berntsen, a former CIA officer who led the team tasked with finding Bin Laden, later claimed the al-Qaeda leader could have indeed been captured if the United States Central Command, headed at the time by Army General Tommy Franks, had given them the troops they had requested to get the job done.

Since then, it has been noted publicly by some of those who fought at Tora Bora that lack of mission support is only partially to blame for Osama's escape. The lion's share of the credit belongs to those who held the mistaken notion that Pakistan was effectively guarding its own border.

Pakistan, our ally in the War on Terror.

Pakistan, the very same country where seven other major al-Qaeda figures have since been found to be hiding. They are:

March 2002: Saudi national Abu Zubaydah, considered to be a close aide of Bin Laden and al-Qaeda's Director of Communications and international operations.

September 2002: Ramzi Bin al-Shibh, suspected of attacking the American warship USS Cole in 1998, arrested in the southern coastal city of Karachi.

March 2003: Khalid Sheikh Mohammed, al-Qaeda's second-in-command, arrested near the Pakistani capital of Islamabad.

July 2004: Ahmed Khalfan Ghailani, suspected of planning of attacks on the U. S. embassy in Kenya. He was handed over to American authorities after Pakistani forces picked him up in the eastern border city of Gujrat.

May 2005: Abu Faraj al-Libi, who at the time was al-Qaida's top man in Pakistan and is allegedly responsible for planning a 2006 plot to detonate liquid explosives carried on board at least ten airplanes travelling from the United Kingdom.

Increased Predator strikes used in Pakistan's northwestern tribal region took the lives of two other al-Qaeda leaders. Abu Lais al-Libi in 2008. Mustafa Al Yazid in 2010. Both blown to bits by drones.

Pakistan. Pakistan. Pakistan.

All five of the al-Qaeda leaders who had been arrested were captured in highly populated urban areas.

Karachi is Pakistan's largest city. Islamabad, the nation's capital.

Raise your hand if you see a pattern here.

As far as anyone knew, Bin Laden had slipped into northwest Pakistan and had been reduced to living in caves to evade capture. By late 2005, U.S. Intelligence intercepted a letter from Atiyah Abd al-Rahman, a senior member of al-Qaeda, to Abu Musab al-Zarquawi, a Jordani militant Islamist known to run a paramilitary training camp in Afghanistan for terrorist recruits. The message instructed Zarqawi to, "Send messengers from your end to Waziristan so that they meet with the brothers of the leadership... I am now on a visit to them and I am writing you this letter as I am with them..."

If Bin Laden was indeed in Waziristan, and there was little reason to believe he wasn't, finding him on Pakistani soil in a lawless mountain region lorded over by tribal leaders and Taliban fighters sympathetic to al-Qaeda anti-Western sentiments would be more difficult than ever.

In early 2009, satellite-aided geographical analysis pointed to three compounds in Parachinar as the most-likely locations where Bin Laden was hiding. However, within the span of just a few months, the hunt for Bin Laden moved north to the Chitral District, Pakistan's most northerly region. Captured al-Qaeda leaders had given up confirmation that this was where the al-Qaeda chief was holed up. The manhunt continued. Patrols sent out in constant search turned up nothing.

Then in December, a Taliban detainee in Pakistan claimed Bin Laden had slipped back into Afghanistan. Days later, frustrated U.S. Secretary of Defense, Robert Gates, publicly stated the joint military forces had no reliable information on the whereabouts of their elusive target. The ghost continued to stay steps ahead of his pursuers even as the War on Terror raged on.

By this time, rumors had been circulating for years that Bin Laden's health, due to kidney failure, had been fading.. Some, including Pakistani leaders, even boldly claimed the al-Qaeda leader had gone to his final reward. Speculation over Bin Laden's death was bolstered by how his sporadic videotaped warnings to America in which he'd begun to look haggard and almost frail, had given way to audiotapes released by his minions featuring a voice possibly not even belonging to the al-Qaeda leader.

For all we knew, he had gone up a mountain and vanished into thin air.

But in the end, Osama Bin Laden, mastermind behind 9/11 and the August 7, 1998, bombings of the United States Embassies in Dar es Salaam, Tanzania, and Nairobi, Kenya, among other acts of murder against innocent civilians, was not only alive, but living well. Contrary to popular belief, he was not cowering in a primitive cave like an animal, but instead hiding in an affluent Pakistani suburb inside a million dollar mansion built behind eighteen-foot high concrete walls topped with barbed wire.

The world's most wanted fugitive had eluded capture by hiding almost in plain sight.

ABBOTTABAD

Welcome to a city of ninety thousand people; a lush, touristy suburb situated in the Orash Valley just an hour's drive north of the Pakistani capital of Islamabad. Sitting at an altitude of forty-one hundred feet, the air is thin and the summers warm. Since colonial times, Abbottabad has been a major transit point to all major tourist regions of Pakistan. In fact, tourism makes up one of the largest portions of the local economy.

Abbottabad is also the home of the Pakistani Military Academy, referred to by some as the Pakistani West Point. As such, it is also a very popular town for former Pakistani military officials to retire in relative comfort.

It is also worth noting that Bin Laden, chosen enemy of the West and all things having to do with western culture, chose as his hiding place, a town founded by a British major, James Abbott, back in 1853.

It was here in Abbottabad that the CIA tracked a courier down a dirt road to a sprawling hilltop compound eight times larger than any of the other properties in the area. Months earlier, Pakistani operatives working for the U.S. had clandestinely pulled up behind a white Suzuki and took note of its license plate. The unsuspecting driver turned out to be Bin Laden's most trusted connection to the outside world.

Immediately, the rush to discover the truth about that compound was on.

Records and satellite images showed Bin Laden's house had been built in 2005. Though no one is quite sure yet how long the al-Qaeda leader had been living there, it has been speculated Bin Laden had called this acre-wide fortress home for years while many of his foot soldiers still slept in caves in the harsh terrain of Pakistan's mountainous border regions.

The property's previous owner, a doctor named Qazi Mahfooz Ul Haq, claims he sold it to someone named Mohammed Arshad, a sturdily built man with a soul patch below his lower lip and a thick accent indicating he was from Waziristan. The doctor was told the purchase was for "an uncle." In total, Arshad purchased four adjoining plots of land for a total of forty-eight thousand dollars.

Neighbors claimed they knew Mohammed Arshad by a different name, Arshad Khan. However, this name was also an alias as Arshad was definitely not who he seemed to be. Khalid Sheikh Mohammed, al-Qaeda's number two in charge, requested Arshad train Maad al-Quhatani, the man who was to have been the twentieth hijacker on 9/11. Khalid Sheikh Mohammed was also one of the masterminds behind the 9/11 plot and was involved with the murder of American journalist Daniel Pearl. Using an Internet cafe in the middle of Karachi, Pakistan's largest city, Arshad attempted to show al-Quhatani how to communicate with 9/11 financier Mohammed Atta, one of the other nineteen hijackers already living in the United States. However, Arshad must have been a poor teacher because al-Quhatani raised too many eyebrows among immigration officials and was turned away when he tried to enter the U.S. illegally in Orlando, Florida, just eleven days before the attacks.

Documents from Gitmo also show that Arshad was one of the men who was with Bin Laden in Tora Bora before he escaped in December 2001.

This man, who neighbors knew as Arshad, was an al-Qaeda operative of great importance who the al-Qaeda leader trusted with his life. Ultimately, it would be Arshad's white Suzuki that would help the U.S. to pinpoint the whereabouts of Bin Laden in August of 2010.

However, the exact trail that led to Arshad began years earlier. During questioning of al-Qaeda "high value" detainees held inside a secret CIA black prison deep inside Eastern Europe, one tiny detail emerged. Months after being put through waterboarding, a form of what Bush-era intelligence personnel called "enhanced interrogation techniques" and some others describe as "torture," Khalid Sheikh Mohammed (KSM) himself gave up the nicknames of several of Bin Laden's couriers.

Just nicknames, nothing more.

One of those nicknames in particular, "al-Kuwaiti," became of great interest to the CIA upon being mentioned again in 2004 by Hassan Ghul, a top al-Qaeda operative arrested in Iraq. Ghul told authorities that al-Kuwaiti was indeed someone crucial to the terrorist organization and was close to al-Qaeda's Director of Operations, Abu Faraj al-Libi.

The following year, U.S. agents intercepted a cell phone call made by al-Libi that allowed them to pinpoint his location on the outskirts of Mardan, some seventy miles northwest of Islamabad. Pakistani authorities were tipped off. They ambushed al-Libi, who had been riding with a driver on a motorbike, and apprehended him, even as he tried in vain to destroy a coded notebook he had been carrying.

Under interrogation, Abu Faraj al-Libi claimed that when he was promoted to succeed KSM as al-Qaeda's operational leader, the order came via courier. U.S. Intelligence officials speculated that a promotion of such magnitude could only have been given to al-Libi by the man in charge, Osama Bin Laden.

This courier was how Bin Laden maintained contact with the outside world. The problem was figuring out the true identity of the one man who could lead them to their target.

With still only a nickname to go with, the lead appeared to be akin to finding a needle in a haystack.

Again, they went back to the data. There had to be something.

Using years of raw intelligence work, in 2007 U.S. Intelligence eventually deduced that the courier was Sheikh Abu Ahmed, a Pakistani man born in Kuwait. Problem was, Ahmed was nowhere to be found and nobody on the U.S. Intelligence payroll could ascertain where this mid-level al-Qaeda operative might be hiding.

While being questioned about Ahmed's whereabouts, one Gitmo detainee claimed Ahmed had suffered fatal wounds fleeing U.S. military forces in Afghanistan and later died in his arms. A claim that, of course, proved to be yet another lie told under the duress of enhanced interrogation.

It was two years later, only after a U.S. wiretap on a known al-Qaeda member turned up a conversation with Ahmed that the trail finally picked up again. With this one phone call, U.S. Intelligence now knew the geographic location where Ahmed and his brother, also an al-Qaeda courier, were operating. Once Ahmed's license plate had been tagged by the CIA, constant surveillance was placed on him. Investigators crossed their fingers and hoped Ahmed would lead them to pay dirt.

For months, they waited and watched, using drones, satellites and surveillance on the ground. Finally the breakthrough they had been hoping for arrived as they tracked Ahmed right to the front door of the Abbottabad compound he purchased under the name of Mohammed Arshad.

CIA analysts began to comb through intelligence reports and satellite photos of the peculiar house to ascertain the identities of those inside. This place was far too large and too extravagant to be housing just a lowly courier.

One thing quickly stood out. Despite its location in what is regarded as an affluent community, and a property value of more than one million dollars, the home had neither an Internet nor a telephone connection.

Another odd thing noted by surveillance of the property was that all the household trash was being routinely burned. It was a small detail that probably wouldn't have seemed so darned suspicious if it hadn't been for the fact that everyone else in the neighborhood just put their trash by the curb.

Investigators wondered, was it a safe house? And if so, for whom?

Certain odd physical details about the residence, including a seven-foot-tall privacy wall obscuring a third-floor balcony from view, pointed toward the house being used to hide someone. Someone say like, Osama Bin Laden who measured at least six feet, four inches in height.

The Abbottabad compound was fishier than week old trout and the CIA began licking its lips over what it had found through good old-fashioned detective work. There could be little doubt from the circumstantial evidence that, at the very least, they had discovered another extremely high-value al-Qaeda target. How high up the wanted-terrorist food chain though, was still anyone's guess.

Aerial surveillance was called in. An array of unmanned drones and satellites kept a watchful eye twenty-four hours a day, tracking who was coming in and out. Those feeds were then continuously downloaded to an Air Force ground station at Langley Air Force Base in Virginia, where even more analysts pored over the data and streamed it live to intelligence officers with the National Counterterrorism Center.

The NCTC, housed in an office complex just across the Potomac River from Washington D.C., worked with the military's Joint Special Operations Command Targeting and Analysis Center, and with the National Geospatial-Intelligence Agency to develop several four-dimensional renderings of the compound. They scanned over every photo, every frame of video, to create a profile of who was living there and what their daily patterns were.

What was later discovered about the compound was that it had been designed and built with deception in mind. Barricades and false walls on every floor were created to bewilder potential intruders. A door, masquerading as the main entrance of the complex, opened only to brick wall.

By September, the CIA began operating under the assumption of a "strong possibility" that hiding inside this mini fortress was none other than Osama Bin Laden himself.

Though many more months of intelligence work would follow to ascertain the exact identity of the high-value al-Qaeda target located in the compound, the CIA meticulously ran and reran the raw data trying to decode the mystery of the Abbottabad house. There had been little doubt from the beginning that the compound was built to protect a major terrorist figure. Surveillance revealed two families living there, but it was satellite images that depicted a third group, one whose size and makeup matched the Bin Laden family.

Senior intelligence officials pegged the chances of this being their man at fifty percent at best.

By February 2011, this intelligence along with that culled from multiple sources including those from CIA "red teams" on the ground, made the picture clear enough to President Obama. The Commander-in-Chief decided an aggressive course of action would indeed be required to bring down this most-hated enemy of all Americans everywhere.

At first, the plan to kill Bin Laden involved targeting him through an air strike on the compound. Two B-2 stealth bombers would drop a few dozen one-ton JDAMs (Joint Direct Attack Munitions) reducing the compound to little more than a pile of rubble inside a gaping crater. However, President Obama was wary of this idea, fearing all the evidence inside would be destroyed as well as their ability to positively identify their man. Notwithstanding, the potential for collateral damage was high given the twenty-two people cited living inside the compound, including women and children. Bin Laden had been responsible for enough innocent casualties. It was the President's desire that no non-combatants be harmed unnecessarily.

However, it would be wrong to categorize this reticence to pull the trigger at first sight as a failure to act on Obama's part. The intel coming in was constantly being revised until the White House was certain they could execute a flawless attack. Predator drone strikes on the target, like the ones used to take out al-Qaeda operatives Abu Lais al-Libi back in 2008 and Mustafa Al Yazid just months earlier in May 2010, were also quickly ruled out. This was an operation requiring pinpoint accuracy and

Obama wanted Bin Laden to face his killers and look them in the eye.

The President and his team then asked the mission be revised to allow for a Special Forces unit to enter the compound by helicopter. Obama instructed CIA Director and Obama nominee for Secretary of Defense, Leon Panetta to proceed under Title 50, meaning this would be the most tight-lipped of covert operations with zero margin for error. Only one team of elite warriors could handle a job of this magnitude; the Joint Special Operations Command or JSOC.

Based out of Pope Air Force Base and Fort Bragg in North Carolina, JSCO was established in 1980 after the devastating failure of U.S. Special Forces to rescue American hostages being held captive at the Iranian embassy during Operation Eagle Claw. JSOC is made up of a highly classified, handpicked group that can only be described as the "best of the best." Among them are the top U.S. Army's Rangers and Delta Force, Naval Special Warfare Development Group and 160th Special Operations Aviation Regiment, a.k.a. the "Night Stalkers." These are the soldiers tasked with performing counterterrorism strike operations and reconnaissance in hostile territory often far behind enemy lines. What in military jargon is often referred to as "denied areas."

These are the men who refuse to be denied.

It's a duty that requires constant risk to one's life without recognition for one's work, all for the pitiful annual salary of about fifty-four thousand dollars. That, my friends, is less than the average schoolteacher earns in a year.

It would be up to a team of Navy SEALS to "find, fix and finish" (intelligence community shorthand for a black bag op) Bin Laden in a highly effective and ruthless surgical strike worthy of any summer tent-pole blockbuster spy movie. However, Jack Ryan or Jack Bauer this is not.

Originally known as SEAL Team Six, the United States Naval Special Warfare Development Group (DevGru) would be the ones tapped to bring Osama Bin Laden to justice. Like its ops undertaken in hostile territory, the details of DevGru are kept highly secret. All potential members are subjected to grueling training at the Naval Special Warfare Center (NSWC), Coronado, California. Graduates of Basic Underwater Demolition School/SEAL (BUD/S) where a twenty-five-week curriculum pushes each candidate to the brink of their mental, physical and emotional endurance. Beyond just becoming a SEAL,

DevGru candidates receive advanced instruction in counterterrorism techniques and explosive ordinance disposal before undergoing a rigorous selection process.

Still, there were those among the senior White House staff who believed bombing the compound was their best bet to get Bin Laden. Known to only stay in one place for short periods of time, the concern was great that if they didn't act quickly, they could lose the al-Qaeda leader to the wind yet again.

However, Obama was undeterred. Navy SEALs had rescued American freighter captain Richard Phillips from Somali pirates back in April of 2009. Held openly in a boat with an AK-47 barrel pressed to the back of his head for five days, Phillips' captors were all killed simultaneously by SEAL sharpshooters firing from more than one hundred feet away on rolling seas.

Three shots, each one piercing the skull of a different Somali pirate in perfect sync.

Obama had all the confidence a surgical strike could be executed. The decision was risky. At home, the President had not endeared himself to those who pointedly repeated the criticism that he had been softer on terror than his predecessor. This would be the biggest decision of his term so far. If this mission failed, he would wear the stigma for the remainder of history, much like Jimmy Carter had for the failure to rescue those American Embassy hostages in Iran.

Under orders from the Commander in Chief, JSOC would begin training for a surgical black bag mission. A strike team of special operators was assembled. As soon as they were given the name of their intended target and told their job was to kill him, a cheer broke out from everyone in the room.

A replica of the one-acre compound was built at Camp Alpha, a segregated section of Bagram Air Base in Afghanistan. Dress rehearsals for this most secret of covert missions began in early April. For two weeks, DevGru practiced two to three times a night, dropping into what would possibly be a very dangerous situation, not knowing exactly what would be waiting for them when they got there, or if their mission would result in success or death.

Back home, Obama's team reiterated this was in no way a slam dunk. The President pondered the possible worst-case scenarios: civilian casualties, a hostage situation, worsening our already tenuous relationship with Pakistan, whom it seemed like was an ally now in name-only.

Three options were put forth on the table: wait and gather more intel, attack from the ground or strike from the air. There was no consensus. John Brennan, the President's senior counter-terrorism adviser, made it known he favored an immediate ground strike. The room was divided down the middle.

Obama told his advisors he would sleep on it. The next morning, Friday April twenty-nine, at eight twenty a.m., before leaving on a busy day of travel with three stops in two states, the President gave the final go-ahead to eliminate Osama Bin Laden.

CODE NAME: GERONIMO

National Security Advisor Tom Donilon received the President's signed orders in the Diplomatic Room of the White House and set the mission for a Saturday launch. However, weather conditions, crucial for the helicopters to enter and exit the target area safely, were poor. The mission would have to be delayed.

During the next seventy-two tense hours, Obama displayed a remarkable poker face. In Alabama, Obama and the First Lady got an up-close look at communities in Tuscaloosa that had been devastated earlier in the week by fierce tornados. Later in the day, the President and his family visited Cape Canaveral, Florida. Originally there to watch the Space Shuttle Endeavor's final journey into space, the launch had to be scrubbed due to technical issues. Undeterred, the First Family toured NASA's facilities and Obama met in private with Gabrielle Giffords, the Arizona Congresswoman who had miraculously survived an assassination attempt earlier in the year, and her astronaut spouse, Mark Kelly, the Endeavor mission commander.

That night, before returning to Washington, Obama even delivered the commencement address at Miami Dade College. In a deeply personal speech, the President sidestepped many of the inspirational phrases he is best known for in favor of recalling his father's troubled life and journey to the U.S. in search of a better education.

"I didn't know him well, my father," said the President. "But I know that when he was around your age, he dreamed of something more than his lot in life. He dreamed of that magical place; he dreamed of coming to study in America."

On Saturday, Obama attended the annual White House Correspondents' Association dinner, a lively event that placed the President square in the middle of a room filled with every reporter and news correspondent who calls the White House beat home. Obama was unflappable and even managed to deliver a few well-deserved zingers at Donald Trump after having endured weeks of pointless attacks by

"The Donald" over the non-issue of the President's Hawaiian birth certificate. One amazing moment happened that evening when comedian and event emcee, Seth Meyers, cracked a joke about the long-sought after Osama Bin Laden.

"People think Bin Laden is hiding in the Hindu Kush," unknowingly quipped Meyers, "but did you know that every day from four to five p.m. he hosts a show on C-SPAN?"

The President's only reaction was a hearty guffaw.

Half a world away, in Abbottabad, morning was rising. It would be the last one of Osama Bin Laden's life. Had he stepped out onto that third-floor balcony, the one behind the seven-foot tall spy wall, and looked upward, he would have seen a beautiful clear sky.

One with plenty of visibility.

Unbeknownst to the al-Qaeda leader, the most hunted man in U.S. history, there were crews fueling helicopters, men readying their weapons and technicians packing their gear. All to come visit him. A man who's codename for this mission would be "Geronimo."

Hours later, in Washington D.C., as was his normal Sunday morning custom, President Obama went to play golf at Andrews Air Force Base. A chilly rain fell as he shot only nine holes instead of his regular eighteen. All in all, Obama spent four hours at Andrews while inside the White House Situation Room, the principles of the mission assembled to prepare.

Around two p.m. EDT, President Obama met with his top advisors one last time to review and ratify the final orders, to dot the last I's and cross the last T's. With the riskiest move of his presidency at hand, Obama signaled he was still all in.

The President returned to the White House Situation Room for an additional briefing at three thirty-two. Even at this point, they still lacked the confirmation to eliminate any doubt Bin Laden would even be there when his guests arrived. Back at Langley, intel from the latest up-to-the-minute satellite images was being examined. Eighteen minutes later, at exactly ten minutes before four, they had an answer. Sort of.

The President was told that Bin Laden had been "tentatively identified." It wasn't like Bin Laden was going to send a postcard or a text message saying, "Yo bitches, I'm here." Though no one, especially Panetta, was one hundred percent sure, this was as much confirmation as they could hope for that Geronimo was in the building. A single satellite image depicting a man who could have been Bin Laden pacing the compound was their best evidence to date.

Langley kept crunching the intel. At one minute past seven, Obama was given a "high probability" that the high value target inside the Abbottabad compound was indeed their man.

There in the Situation Room of the White House, Commander in Chief Obama gathered with Brigadier General Marshall B. "Brad" Webb, Assistant Commanding General, Joint Special Operations Command; Deputy National Security Advisor Denis McDonough; Secretary of State Hillary Rodham Clinton; Secretary of Defense Robert Gates; Admiral Mike Mullen, Chairman of the Joint Chiefs of Staff; National Security Advisor Tom Donilon; Chief of Staff Bill Daley; Tony Binken, National Security Advisor to the Vice President; Audrey Tomason, Director for Counterterrorism; John Brennan, Assistant to the President for Homeland Security and Counterterrorism; and Director of National Intelligence James Clapper.

Simultaneously, Panetta created a private communications center in his personal conference room at Langley. From there, he took direct command of the military team responsible for the assault and the analysts monitoring from afar.

Panetta, who was responsible for relaying information to the White House, was himself getting his feed directly from Vice Adm. William McRaven, head of the Joint Special Forces Command, in Afghanistan. On the ground, this was McRaven's operation. Any direct contact with the assault team would be coming from McRaven, if needed.

Though the SEALs were equipped with helmet-cams recording video, McRaven, back in Afghanistan, would only be privy to the team's radio feeds. This audio would be only for him to hear. Everything Panetta learned about the mission's progress in real-time would come from McRaven and it would be Panetta's responsibility to daisy-chain it on up to the White House. It was like a game of *Whisper Down the Lane*, with the exception that in this case, someone was going to die.

At one fifteen a.m. Afghanistan time, two helicopters took off from Bagram, one hundred sixty miles from Bin Laden's compound. Twenty-five SEALs rode in a pair of modified Black Hawk MH-60s stealth helicopters. One quick stop was made in Jalalabad to pick up their escorts: two Chinook MH-47s loaded with a back-up force of men and extra fuel just in case it was needed. Attached to the MH-60s were stealth-configured shapes on the boom and tip fairings, swept stabilizers and a "dishpan" cover over a non-standard five blade tail rotor, all designed to reduce the helicopter's radar signature. Other aerodynamic modifications, along with flight control adjustments, would allow for a reduced rotor speed and less noise, further making these Black Hawks impossible to detect as they crept across the Pakistani border in the dead of night.

From this point there was no turning back. Back in Washington came the biggest shocker of all, Obama's team had elected to tell no one. We were about to execute an assassination mission on Pakistani soil without their approval or even their knowledge. If everything went "tits up," this would be the kind of international incident that would be virtually impossible to smooth over by sending over a bouquet of flowers and a muffin basket.

Two and a half kilometers away from an infamous neighbor he never knew he had, a thirty-three-year-old programmer named Sohaib Athar noticed something peculiar in the sky. A helicopter was hovering over his neighborhood, something that was not a common event for Abbottabad.

Not knowing he would then be the only person in the world live-blogging about the assault, he sent the following Tweet: *Go away helicopter - before I take out my giant swatter :-/ "*

Much like the rest of the world, Sohib Athar, the man who would become the most famous Pakistani Twitter user ever, had no idea what would happen next. As it turned out, even the SEALs best laid plans were going slightly astray.

Originally, one group of raiders was to be dropped into the compound's main courtyard. A second group of SEALs would then "fast rope" onto the roof of the main building, a technique developed by U.K. troops in the Falklands War. During fast-roping, soldiers slide down using only gloved hands and their own feet. It is quick but dangerous, especially when wearing a combat pack on your back and trying to avoid being shot.

Trouble came quickly and unexpectedly as the second helicopter's rotors suddenly lost lift in the hot high altitude air over the compound. Fighting for control of the stick, the pilot was able to land the bird gently in the courtyard despite clipping the tail rotor on a wall. The pilot tried to restart the engine with no luck. The Black Hawk was dead.

Back in the White House situation room, things grew tense. Surely running through everyone's mind was the fear of another *Black Hawk Down* scenario; brave boys having to fight for their lives, stuck behind enemy lines without a ride home.

Lost now was the element of surprise. Between the raiders and the compound was an inner ring of walls. The SEALs were going to have to blast their way in. Lead came flying the moment the first men hit the compound. Hostile fire came quickly, provided by the surprised and half-asleep courier and his brother stumbling out into the night with weapons drawn. Osama's handful of ragtag protectors were outgunned and outclassed by the vastly more heavily trained SEALs wearing night-vision goggles and armed with combat-ready and suppressor-enabled AR-15 assault rifles.

From above, the remaining hovering Black Hawk and the Chinooks provided a lookout platform as the assault raged below. On the ground, SEALs outflanked the little resistance they met and easily pushed forward to the main dwelling to reach Bin Laden. Intelligence sources had pinpointed the al-Qaeda leader was most likely living on the second and third floors of the largest structure.

Sweeping through the fortress-like grounds, SEALs had anticipated the possibility of deadly booby traps or IEDs, so a specially trained dog was brought to help sniff out any explosives.

Intel had revealed more than two dozen women and children living at the compound. At every turn, life and death calls had to be made over who was lethal and who was just in the way. From the Middle Eastern conflicts of the last two decades, U.S. forces knew anybody could potentially be armed with a suicide vest laden with explosives. As they advanced, SEALs used plastic zip ties to handcuff every adult they came across before ushering them to a holding area out of harm's way. In all, twenty-three children were found. None were hurt.

Twenty-five minutes into the mission, Panetta sill had no word from McRaven. The President and his team huddled in the West Wing of the White House anxiously waiting for updates that weren't coming. The roll of the dice Obama had made on this mission was threatening to come up snake eyes.

SEALs penetrated into the main building, checking inside closets and under beds, shouting "clear" as each room was deemed safe for entry. A small arsenal of guns was uncovered and immediately confiscated. The raiders stormed up the stairs, certain their quarry was within reach.

"It was probably the most anxiety-filled periods of time," John Brennan later told reporters during a White House briefing the morning after the assault. "The minutes passed like days, and the President was very concerned about the security of our personnel."

Then came the words they had been hoping for: "Visual on Geronimo." Bin Laden had been spotted.

As the SEALS burst into a third floor bedroom, a woman charged at them, crying out her husband's name. It was Bin Laden's youngest wife, Amal Ahmed Abdul Fatah, a Yemeni native who, as a fifteen-year-old, had been given to the al-Qaeda leader as a gift by her tribal family. The now twenty-nine-year-old Amal, lived in the compound with Bin Laden and their three children, a daughter and two sons. In a fury, she rushed one of the SEALs in a futile attempt to protect her husband and was shot in the leg, but not killed. Fearing she may be wearing a suicide vest, she was dragged away from the room. From across the hall, Bin Laden and Amal's thirteen- year-old daughter witnessed everything.

Though vastly outnumbered, Bin Laden resisted capture. He made a threatening move, assumed to be an attempt to reach one of the AK-47s later found in the bedroom. Unfortunately for the al-Qaeda leader, that move ended up being his last. A split-second decision by at least one of the SEALs to fire, resulted in Bin Laden taking two bullets; one slug to the chest and another to the left eye, blowing away part of his skull.

The once-mighty leader of the world's most-feared terrorist organization lay dead in his own bedroom with this blood and brains leaking onto the floor.

Even though they had heard Amal shout out Bin Laden's name, positive identification was still necessary. The SEALs had come fully prepared for any contingency, but the one thing none of the raiders brought was a tape measure to size up the famously tall Bin Laden. Improvising, one of the SEALs lay down next to Bin Laden's corpse to ascertain that the man they had just killed was approximately six-foot four inches in height. Moments later, a gruesome photograph of the body was taken digitally and uploaded to a facial recognition program.

Back at the White House, the President tensely awaited news. Had years of intel and guesswork finally paid off or had they gone down the rabbit hole and found nothing? Finally, a coded message came across the radio from the SEAL team, "Geronimo-E KIA."

E stood for "enemy" and KIA for "Killed in Action."

"We got him," said the President.

When the smoke cleared, several enemy combatants had been killed including the courier Abu Ahmed, his brother, Bin Laden's twenty-two-year-old son, Khalid, and a woman later identified as Ahmed's wife, who had been caught in the crossfire.

Not one single U.S. casualty was suffered in the assault.

While scrubbing Bin Laden's compound for evidence of possible future terrorist attacks, the SEAL team turned up a treasure trove of intel. Ten cell phones, ten computers and more than a hundred different thumb drives were confiscated during the forty-minute raid.

One can only imagine what was on Osama Bin Laden's computer.

Up to the very last, Bin Laden had prepared for the possibility of a hasty escape. Sewn into his clothing were five hundred Euros and two secret phone numbers.

By now the assault team had long overstayed their welcome. It was time for a hasty and improvised exit. McRaven gave the orders to destroy the damaged helicopter. Explosives were quickly placed inside the damaged stealth Black Hawk and detonated. One of the Chinooks landed on the street. Quickly, the SEALs were forced to carry Bin Laden's body out on foot; a decidedly humiliating ending for a man who swore he would never be taken dead or alive by American forces.

MISSION ACCOMPLISHED

From Abbottabad, the corpse of the most wanted man in U.S. intelligence history was flown back to Afghanistan for positive identification. Several years earlier, Osama's sister had died of brain cancer in a hospital in Boston, Massachusetts. Her body had been immediately subpoenaed by the FBI so that it could be later used to identify the al-Qaeda leader if he was ever caught. Tissue samples taken from her brain provided a ninety-nine point ninety-seven percent match to the DNA of the man the SEAL team had killed.

Though there will surely be conspiracy theorists who will forever claim Bin Laden was taken alive to be interrogated or tortured in some CIA secret prison, never to see the light of day, perhaps the most telling evidence was the fact that nobody from al-Qaeda disputed their leader had been killed.

There should be zero doubt. Osama Bin Laden is dead.

In Islam, the dead are generally buried in the ground, without a casket, before the next of five daily prayer periods have passed. The White House feared that giving the world's most infamous terrorist a known grave would be too risky so they opted to disposed of Bin Laden's corpse somewhere it could never be located.

The Indian Ocean.

Bin Laden was placed aboard the aircraft carrier USS Carl Vinson, where the body was transported to its final resting place. A Muslim seaman from the U.S. Navy recited the prayers and ensured the body was washed and wrapped in a cloth in accordance to religious custom. Shortly past one a.m. am EDT, on May 2, 2011, Bin Laden's bullet-riddled corpse was given a burial at sea.

Osama Bin Laden's death is a major blow to the organization he helped found. His loss is immeasurable. He was a charismatic leader who was not only responsible for masterminding terrorism against the West but a figurehead in the fundraising efforts from sympathizers from around the world. Sure, the al-Qaeda loyalists, the small group of fanatical fighters who swore their allegiance to Bin Laden's crusade, remains active, but U.S.-led coalition forces have been chipping away at their ranks over recent years, killing important lieutenants with drone strikes and capturing others. With al-Qaeda's experienced and skilled leaders being removed from the equation at a rapid pace, along with growing counterintelligence operations being pursued to flush their operatives out of hiding, can this radical wing of anti-American extremists survive?

The vast amount of intel taken from Bin Laden's residence could also signal the death knell to al-Qaeda's future. The mobile phones and thumb drives were most likely used by the two couriers to carry data back and forth to al-Qaeda operatives in the outside world. Counterterrorism technicians will trace the phone numbers found and hard drives will be meticulously searched for clues. They will sift through every bit and byte of data for mentions of explosives or keywords such as "weddings," often used by al-Qaeda to signify a bombing.

It is certain the operation to kill Osama Bin Laden will go down as a major U.S. military victory and the greatest terrorist manhunt in history. After the mission, retired U.S. Army General Barry McCaffrey called JSOC "the most dangerous people on the face of the earth." There is no reason whatsoever to question the veracity of this claim.

Yet, some say the killing of Osama Bin Laden will not destroy al-Qaeda, nor will it paralyze its fanatical followers. This is not the equivalent of dropping the atom bomb on Hiroshima. Our foes may be deeply injured, but it does not mean they have been fully vanquished.

Less than a week after the assault, al-Qaeda on one of the radical Islamic militant websites known to post messages from its leaders reportedly vowed revenge.

"The blood of the holy warrior sheik, Osama bin Laden, God bless him, is too precious to us and to all Muslims to go in vain," the statement read in part. "We will remain, God willing, a curse chasing the Americans and their agents, following them outside and inside their countries."

In the wake of Bin Laden's killing, many questions remain.

Although this suburban sprawl of Abbottabad is home to many retired members of the Pakistani military command, and Bin Laden's own bedroom was situated less than one mile from the Pakistani Military Academy, it may never be clear how much Pakistan knew about Bin Laden's whereabouts. In the days following Bin Laden's death, some speculated the compound at Abbottabad had also been home to a guesthouse frequently used by Pakistani intelligence agencies.

What effect this covert raid and the secrets that may be revealed will have with America's relationship with Pakistan is unsure. As an ally, can they be trusted?

From 9/11 to Osama Bin Laden's death, the United States spent nearly one point four trillion dollars on the War on Terror. Thousands of brave young men and women have given their lives in the name of Liberty.

In the end, was it worth the cost?

The gut punch Osama Bin Laden landed on 9/11 still stings. What he took from our country on that terrible day can never be replaced, nor can the lives of the thousands of innocent men, women and children murdered in the name of some crusade. And even though it will still be a long time until we Americans fully heal from the pain of the worst terrorist attacks on our soil, we can rest assured that the man who became the epitome of evil in the modern world will never do this again.

It is difficult to deny the value of Bin Laden's death on a wounded America. Even the seventy-five-year-old Dalai Lama implied that the killing of Osama Bin Laden was justified.

"Forgiveness doesn't mean forget what happened," the holy leader told a crowd at USC just days after the killing, also adding that sometimes you have to take counter measures.

Though Bin Laden is survived by at least eighteen children, it is believed that none of his sons ever played any real operational roles in al-Qaeda or were groomed to in any way succeed their father as the head of the world's most notorious terrorist organization.

Are there any young like-minded radicals out there willing to take Osama Bin Laden's place as the leader of al-Qaeda's jihad against the West? Truth is there are dozens, if not hundreds. There also has been much speculation that al-Qaeda may soon see the base of its operations move to Yemen where sympathies for its cause run deep. Only time will tell whether we have cut the head off of the snake or just one of the many heads of the hydra.

Still, there is also reason to believe al-Qaeda is already running scared. Just three days after Bin Laden's death was announced to the world, Khaled Hathal Abdullah al-Atifi, an al-Qaeda operative on many wanted lists, phoned authorities in Pakistan to surrender. Obviously, to al-Atifi, a jail cell was preferable than a bullet to the head.

So if the manhunt for Osama Bin Laden is any indication, all other terrorist enemies of America would best think twice lest they believe they can win this war. For what awaits them is not martyrdom or success, but more than likely, a gruesome death at the hands of U.S. soldiers.

On May fifth, just four days after speaking to the world on live television to announce the death of the man U.S. Military forces had hunted for almost a decade, President Barack Obama flew to New York City and paid a visit to Ground Zero. There he spoke with police officers and firefighters whose brothers were lost on 9/11 along with the two thousand, seven hundred fifty-two people killed in the World Trade Center. There at the site of the attacks, the Commander in Chief somberly laid a wreath patriotically created out of red, white and blue flowers. No grand speech was made. Heads were bowed in prayer and reflection.

"When we say we will never forget, we mean what we say," declared the President.

Though his words held a double-edged meaning, this day was not in any way about the murderer who had been brought to justice, but about the murdered themselves. The American story has always been one of survival and struggle, from our colonial ancestors who founded this land to build a better tomorrow for their children to the men and women who fought to preserve freedom here and overseas.

Mostly the American story is one of remembrance.

We will *never* forget those who were lost.

We can and will survive anything because no matter how hard our enemies may try, they can never kill the indomitable spirit that defines us.

OBAMA'S SPEECH ANNOUNCING THE DEATH OF OSAMA BIN LADEN

Anytime a President speaks, it's a snapshot of history.

And only time will tell if that President's words were true.

On May 1, 2011, at 11:35 p.m. EDT, ironically, sixty-six years to the day after the announcement that Hitler was dead, President Barack Obama gave the following speech live from the East Room of the White House.

THE PRESIDENT: Good evening. Tonight, I can report to the American people and to the world that the United States has conducted an operation that killed Osama Bin Laden, the leader of al-Qaeda, and a terrorist who's responsible for the murder of thousands of innocent men, women, and children.

It was nearly ten years ago that a bright September day was darkened by the worst attack on the American people in our history. The images of 9/11 are seared into our national memory—hijacked planes cutting through a cloudless September sky; the Twin Towers collapsing to the ground; black smoke billowing up from the Pentagon; the wreckage of Flight 93 in Shanksville, Pennsylvania, where the actions of heroic citizens saved even more heartbreak and destruction.

And yet we know that the worst images are those that were unseen to the world. The empty seat at the dinner table. Children who were forced to grow up without their mother or their father. Parents who would never know the feeling of their child's embrace. Nearly three thousand citizens taken from us, leaving a gaping hole in our hearts.

On September 11, 2001, in our time of grief, the American people came together. We offered our neighbors a hand, and we offered the wounded our blood. We reaffirmed our ties to each other, and our love of community and country. On that day, no matter where we came from, what God we prayed to, or what race or ethnicity we were, we were united as one American family.

We were also united in our resolve to protect our nation and to bring those who committed this vicious attack to justice. We quickly learned that the 9/11 attacks were carried out by al-Qaeda—an organization headed by Osama Bin Laden, which had openly declared war on the United States and was committed to killing innocents in our country and around the globe. And so we went to war against al-Qaeda to protect our citizens, our friends, and our allies.

Over the last ten years, thanks to the tireless and heroic work of our military and our counterterrorism professionals, we've made great strides in that effort. We've disrupted terrorist attacks and strengthened our homeland defense. In Afghanistan, we removed the Taliban government, which had given Bin Laden and al-Qaeda safe haven and support. And around the globe, we worked with our friends and allies to capture or kill scores of al-Qaeda terrorists, including several who were a part of the 9/11 plot.

Yet Osama Bin Laden avoided capture and escaped across the Afghan border into Pakistan. Meanwhile, al-Qaeda continued to operate from along that border and operate through its affiliates across the world.

And so shortly after taking office, I directed Leon Panetta, the director of the CIA, to make the killing or capture of Bin Laden the top priority of our war against al-Qaeda, even as we continued our broader efforts to disrupt, dismantle, and defeat his network.

Then, last August, after years of painstaking work by our intelligence community, I was briefed on a possible lead to Bin Laden. It was far from certain, and it took many months to run this thread to ground. I met repeatedly with my national security team as we developed more information about the possibility that we had located Bin Laden hiding within a compound deep inside of Pakistan. And finally, last week, I determined that we had enough intelligence to take action, and authorized an operation to get Osama Bin Laden and bring him to justice.

Today, at my direction, the United States launched a targeted operation against that compound in Abbottabad, Pakistan. A small team of Americans carried out the operation with extraordinary courage and capability. No Americans were harmed. They took care to avoid civilian casualties. After a firefight, they killed Osama Bin Laden and took custody of his body.

For over two decades, Bin Laden has been al-Qaeda's leader and symbol, and has continued to plot attacks against our country and our friends and allies. The death of Bin Laden marks the most significant achievement to date in our nation's effort to defeat al-Qaeda.

Yet his death does not mark the end of our effort. There's no doubt that al-Qaeda will continue to pursue attacks against us. We must —and we will—remain vigilant at home and abroad.

As we do, we must also reaffirm that the United States is not –and never will be– at war with Islam. I've made clear, just as President Bush did shortly after 9/11, that our war is not against Islam. Bin Laden was not a Muslim leader; he was a mass murderer of Muslims. Indeed, al-Qaeda has slaughtered scores of Muslims in many countries, including our own. So his demise should be welcomed by all who believe in peace and human dignity.

Over the years, I've repeatedly made clear that we would take action within Pakistan if we knew where Bin Laden was. That is what we've done. But it's important to note that our counterterrorism cooperation with Pakistan helped lead us to Bin Laden and the compound where he was hiding. Indeed, Bin Laden had declared war against Pakistan as well, and ordered attacks against the Pakistani people.

Tonight, I called President Zardari, and my team has also spoken with their Pakistani counterparts. They agree that this is a good and historic day for both of our nations. And going forward, it is essential that Pakistan continue to join us in the fight against al-Qaeda and its affiliates.

The American people did not choose this fight. It came to our shores, and started with the senseless slaughter of our citizens. After nearly ten years of service, struggle, and sacrifice, we know well the costs of war. These efforts weigh on me every time I, as Commander-in-Chief, have to sign a letter to a family that has lost a loved one, or look into the eyes of a service member who's been gravely wounded.

So Americans understand the costs of war. Yet as a country, we will never tolerate our security being threatened, nor stand idly by when our people have been killed. We will be relentless in defense of our citizens and our friends and allies. We will be true to the values that make us who we are. And on nights like this one, we can say to those families who have lost loved ones to al-Qaeda's terror: Justice has been done.

Tonight, we give thanks to the countless intelligence and counterterrorism professionals who've worked tirelessly to achieve this outcome. The American people do not see their work, nor know their names. But tonight, they feel the satisfaction of their work and the result of their pursuit of justice.

We give thanks for the men who carried out this operation, for they exemplify the professionalism, patriotism, and unparalleled courage of those who serve our country. And they are part of a generation that has borne the heaviest share of the burden since that September day.

Finally, let me say to the families who lost loved ones on 9/11 that we have never forgotten your loss, nor wavered in our commitment to see that we do whatever it takes to prevent another attack on our shores.

And tonight, let us think back to the sense of unity that prevailed on 9/11. I know that it has, at times, frayed. Yet today's achievement is a testament to the greatness of our country and the determination of the American people.

The cause of securing our country is not complete. But tonight, we are once again reminded that America can do whatever we set our mind to. That is the story of our history, whether it's the pursuit of prosperity for our people, or the struggle for equality for all our citizens; our commitment to stand up for our values abroad, and our sacrifices to make the world a safer place.

Let us remember that we can do these things not just because of wealth or power, but because of who we are: one nation, under God, indivisible, with liberty and justice for all.

Thank you. May God bless you. And may God bless the United States of America.

AUTHOR'S NOTE

Some months after the first publication of this book, I received the following email from former British soldier, Chris Harding.

There are many men and women including myself who have fought in far off lands in the name of the War on Terror. There were many nationalities killed in the Twin Towers and there are many families who have lost loved ones since then, but in your book you have focused on America and Americans with very little reference to those who have also been involved. This is not a criticism of your book, but an observation from someone who also has some skin in this game.

Chris is absolutely right. Though the commentary bookending the historic facts surrounding this event is based from my perspective as an American observing the reaction in the U.S., I was rightfully reminded that, from the beginning, this conflict was indeed a global concern that touched the lives of free citizens from all across the globe. The burden of this war waged against the perpetrators of terror has been shared by our many allies. It would be disingenuous to believe it was solely America's fight or only America's victory. The sacrifices made by soldiers and citizens like Chris should be honored as deeply as we would honor our own. Together, we are united as members of a global society that value freedom and liberty. We will never stand for the tyranny of terrorism or the threat to our children's futures in a world better than the one we leave behind.

ACKNOWLEDGEMENTS

This book goes out to the brave men and women of the U.S. military. Your valor and courage make me proud to be an American. Please get home safely.

To American presidents, both present and past, I thank you for suffering through suffocating criticism over your foreign policies. Nobody with half a mind doubts your desire to keep America safe from its enemies. Yours is a job only an insane person would want and I very much appreciate all the things that happen in the Oval Office that are far, far beyond my grasp of understanding.

And to you, Osama Bin Laden…please enjoy an eternity of having your temperature taken with a pitchfork.

The latest exposé from award-winning and bestselling author
Mark Yoshimoto Nemcoff...

FATAL SUNSET
DEADLY VACATIONS

No one ever believes their dream vacation can instantly turn into a tragic nightmare...until it's too late.

Some tourists vanish without a trace. **Over 170 people have disappeared from cruise ships around the world since 1995**, several under very suspicious circumstances. Others have their lives senselessly stolen, like the 8-year old boy sucked into an unprotected pool drain at a major resort, leaving his mother crying out his name as security staff held her at gunpoint. **Or 22-year old Nolan Webster, denied proper medical care after being pulled unconscious from a Cancun resort pool, only to have his dead body left in plain view for hours and his parents billed for his room.**

Vacations are meant to be joyous and fun. Sometimes terrible things happen unexpectedly. **A parasailing newlywed plummets hundreds of feet to her death on the last day of her honeymoon when her harness snaps in mid-air. Hikers make a fatal plunge on an improperly-marked Kauai cliffside trail. And of course, there's every mother's nightmare: the disappearance of Natalee Holloway** while on a high school graduation trip to Aruba with members of her senior class.

"There's one piece of advice I've learned researching this book," tells Nemcoff. **"Dare to be aware."**

BOOKS BY MARK YOSHIMOTO NEMCOFF

NON-FICTION:
- Fatal Sunset: Deady Vacations
- The Killing of Osama Bin Laden: How the Mission to Hunt Down a Terrorist Mastermind was Accomplished
- Where's My F*cking Latte? (And Other Stories About Being an Assistant in Hollywood)
- Go Forth and Kick Some Ass (Be the Hero of Your Own Life Story)
- Pacific Coast Hellway Presents - Pissed Off: Is Better Than Being Pissed On
- Admit You Hate Yourself

FICTION:
- Diary of a Madman
- The Doomsday Club
- The Art of Surfacing
- Number One with a Bullet
- Shadow Falls: Badlands
- Shadow Falls: Angel of Death
- Killing My Boss
- Transistor Rodeo
- INFINITY

ABOUT THE AUTHOR

Mark Yoshimoto Nemcoff is a bestselling and award-winning author who has been known to occasionally moonlight as a voice-over artist and independent journalist. He is a former Sirius Satellite Radio drive time show and T.V. host that has been featured by Playboy Magazine and Access Hollywood. He is the writer behind Kindle bestsellers "The Death of Osama Bin Laden" and "Where's My F***ing Latte?", an insiders look at the world of Hollywood celebrity assistants that was not only featured on Access Hollywood, but has spent over four years straight at the top of Amazon's top-selling chart in the categories of "Television" and "Movies."

Mark currently resides in Los Angeles.

He can be reached at: MYN@WordSushi.com
Twitter.com/MYN
Facebook.com/MYNBooks

If you enjoyed this book, please tell your friends.

-MYN

16009445R00042

Made in the USA
Lexington, KY
29 June 2012